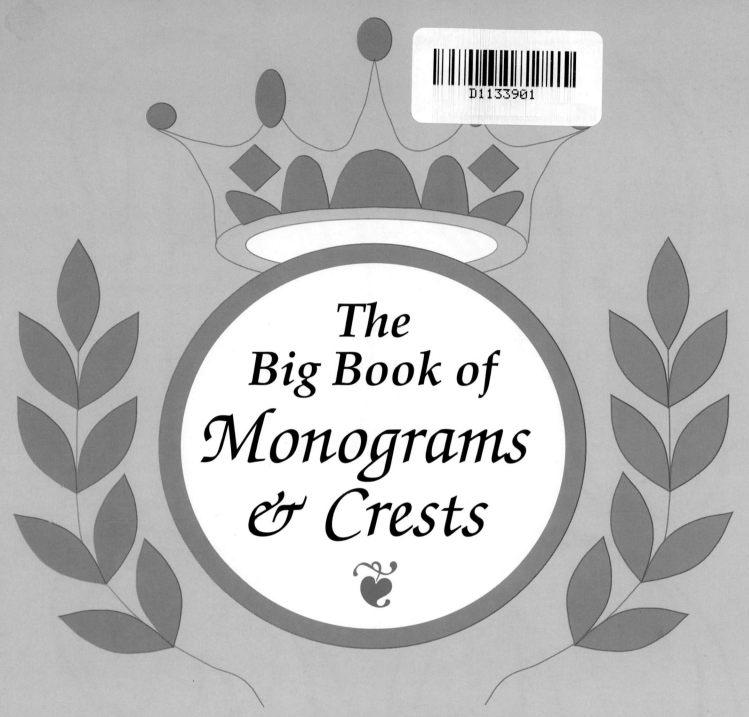

The Big Book of Monograms & Crests

by Barry Geller

Iron-on, reusable, transfer letters and numbers for wearable art and home decorating.

- Easy to transfer • Fun to paint
- Attractive to wear

ISBN 0-937769-77-0 • © 1990 Barry Geller • Photography by Todd Tsukushi • Makeup by Alison Kelsen/Facial Impressions

IRON-ON TRANSFER INSTRUCTIONS

Art-to-wear clothing is simple and fun with this complete iron-on transfer book. All of the basic steps are accompanied by illustrated, step-by-step instructions to help you achieve beautiful effects. You can create attractive clothing and accessories with confidence and perhaps even start your own art-to-wear business!

Before you begin...

- Read all instructions and tips carefully
- Gather materials for project

SUPPLIES

- Iron-on transfer
- Cardboard to fit in shirt
- Sharp scissors
- Squeeze bottle fabric paints

- Iron
- Paper towel or soft cloth
- Ironing board
- Decorative trims such as rhinestones (optional)

- Pre-washed sweatshirt or item to be decorated
- Fabric glue if trim is used

To begin...

- Protect your ironing board cover with a clean cloth
- Pre-wash and dry garment to remove sizing, paint will have a better grip on unsized fabrics.
- Preheat iron to recommended temperature for the fabric you are decorating. DO NOT USE STEAM!

DESIGN TRANSFER

Step 1. Cut out the transfer design carefully. Cut off lines or parts of the design you do not want to transfer.

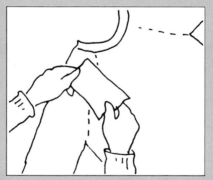

Step 2. Position the selected transfer design in on the right-side of the fabric —INK-SIDE DOWN.

Step 3. Place the preheated iron directly on the transfer pattern. Press and lift an edge of the transfer paper while holding the rest of the design in place. Look to see if the ink has transferred.

DO NOT SLIDE THE IRON THE WAY YOU DO WHEN IRONING—THE DESIGN COULD SMEAR.
Lift the iron directly off the garment and allow the transfer paper to remain in place until cool. Lift the transfer paper off of the garment.

TIP: Transfers can be used more than once, but they get lighter with each use. Use the shortest amount of ironing time possible for a clear transfer and transfer will be reusable! When reusing a transfer design, place a piece of aluminum foil on the ironing board under the fabric; this will allow for a darker transfer of the ink.

TIP: Place a piece of cardboard inside the garment, under the area to be painted. This will prevent paint from bleeding through. Paint along the outlines of the design or fill in the shapes with color. Complete painting instructions are on the pages to follow.

PAINTING INSTRUCTIONS

Transfer ink is not permanent on 100% cotton. On polyester blends, the ink is permanent.

Painting on fabric is easy. Visit your favorite fabric or craft store for the latest in fabric paints. Any type of acrylic paint will work on fabric because it is permanent and holds color beautifully.

Small squeeze bottles of fabric paint are wonderful because there is no need for brushing paint on; simply, squeeze paint from the tube to form lines and fill in the shapes with the bottle tips.

Paints To Try: *These are descriptions, not brand names*

SLICK PAINT - has a glossy plastic finish - gives a bright shiny "wet" look

SHINY PAINT - gives a glossy "wet" look with great colors

PEARLIZED - creates a glowing pearl effect

IRIDESCENT- has a soft shimmering effect, beautiful for floral designs and evening wear.

GLITTERING - glitter is mixed in the paint, this is a great way to have a glittery effect without glitter mess.

GLOW-IN-THE-DARK - paint that absorbes light will glow brightly in the dark. Try it for Halloween and childrens' bedtime clothing and accessories.

FLUORESCENT - for day glow brights & neon color effects

Helpful paint supplies

- Brushes - #4 watercolor
- 1/4 inch flat brush
- Permanent fabric marker pens
- Drop cloth for color wash painting
- Paper towel for wiping the brush
- Cup of clean water for brush cleaning
- Small ceramic dish for a pallet

TIP: Work from the top to the bottom, this will save you from touching wet paint!

Storing Paint:
Store paint with caps on securely. Squeeze bottle paints often get air bubbles, so store them upside down to reduce bubbles.

Painting is easy

- Use fabric paints. They come in squeeze bottles and are easy to use and washable.
- Shake bottle before using.
- Put a piece of heavy paper or cardboard inside the garment for protection.
- Spread the paint with the nozzle of the squeeze bottle or with a brush.
- You can mix the paint to create new colors in a ceramic pallet or dish.
- The paints can be thinned with water.
- If you use a brush, clean it with water.
- Let fabric dry for four hours or use a hair dryer.

COLOR WASH WITH PAINT

Dilute acrylic paint with water and apply to the design with a wet brush... paint will bleed beyond the lines of the transfer design. Allow the color wash to dry and outline with squeeze bottle paints —add freehand strokes to create a loose look. Allow four hours for the paint to completely dry .

Dry painted clothing flat and do not launder garment for 24 hours.

Freehand: Freehand strokes will add life to your design. Practice on paper to loosen up and remember that your strokes make the design an original.

Color Washes: Dilute acrylic or squeeze bottle paints by mixing a 50/50 ratio to water, brush this on with a wet brush. In order to spread the paint, brush over the area while it is still wet by using clean water. You can also spray an area with clean water before color washing to give paint soft edges.

Splash and Splatter: Full strength or diluted paint can be splattered on garment with a paint brush. For a finer effect, dip an old toothbrush into the paint, shake off the excess paint carefully and flick the toothbrush with your thumb. This takes a bit of practice but the effect is great!

Circles: Use a dinner plate to create a perfect circle design. Simply, position the plate in the center of the garment and make small dots with your fabric marker pen. Use the dots as a guide when ironing on the transfer.

Mistakes: There are no mistakes in art but if you have an unplanned drip or dot, try making it into an extra leaf or element of the design. Sometimes adding more dots in that area works well. If the drip or smear is large and cannot be remedied, try using the fusing technique or fabric glue to add a design over the area. A drip can sometimes be removed if sponged at once with warm water.

CREATING DESIGNS ON DARK COLORED FABRICS

Transfer design to light colored fabric and fuse it to a dark colored garment.

In addition to basic supplies, you will need...

• White or a light-colored printed cotton or poly/cotton blend— the design will be ironed to this fabric.
• Fusible webbing or fusible sheeting—follow instructions that are included with the webbing or sheets for proper heat setting.

Note: Fusible webbing or sheets can be purchased at your local fabric store.

If you want to use your iron-on transfer design on denim or dark fabric, simply follow these easy steps:

Step 1. Cut out the selected iron-on transfer design.

Step 2. Follow the transfer instructions and iron the design to a light-colored cotton or poly/cotton blend.

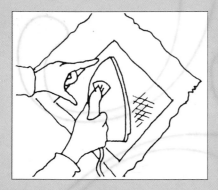

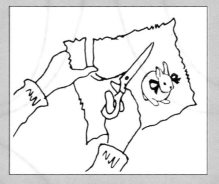

Step 3. Iron fusible sheet to reverse-side of fabric. Be sure all of the design is backed by fusible material.

Step 4. Cut out the iron-on transfer design by following the outside edge of the pattern. Peel the paper backing from the fusible material. Your iron-on transfer is now ready to be placed on denim or dark clothing and be ironed in place.

Step 5. Place the cut out iron-on transfer on denim or dark clothing and iron the design in place.

Step 6. Paint and decorate the design!

ART-TO-WEAR CARE

Hand washing and hanging to dry are the safest ways to clean hand decorated clothing. If you are machine washing, turn the garment inside out or place in a pillow case (twist tie the pillow case closed) and wash on delicate cycle. Machine drying can crack and dry fabric paints. In addition, ironing the painted area is not recommended.

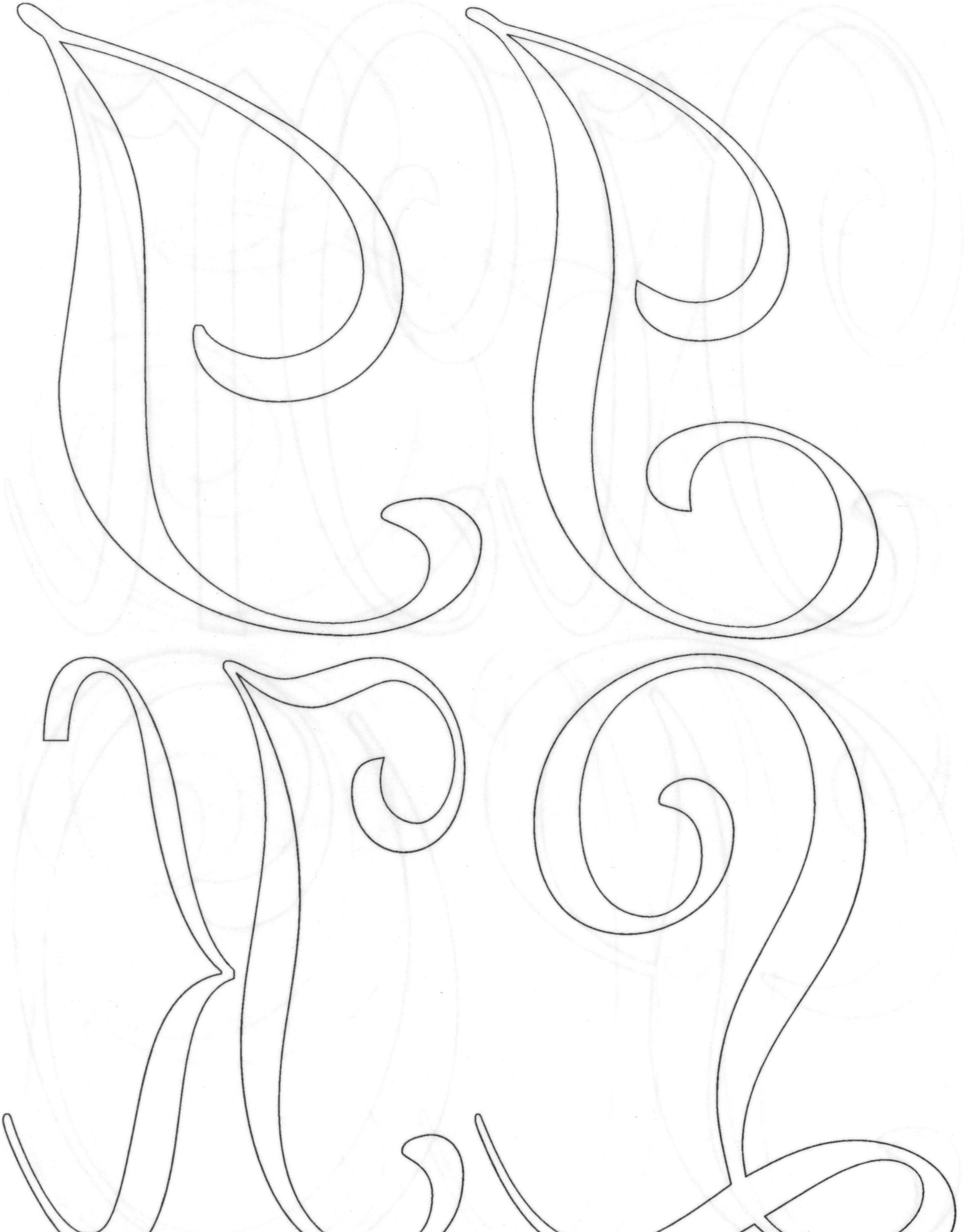

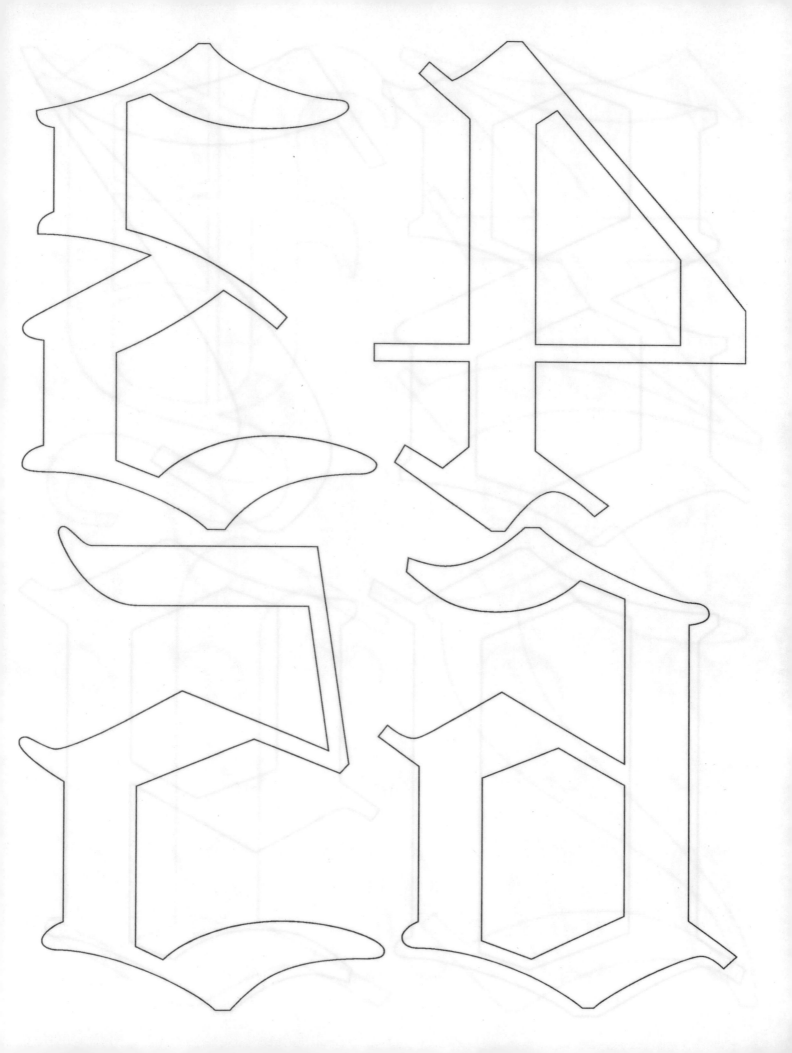

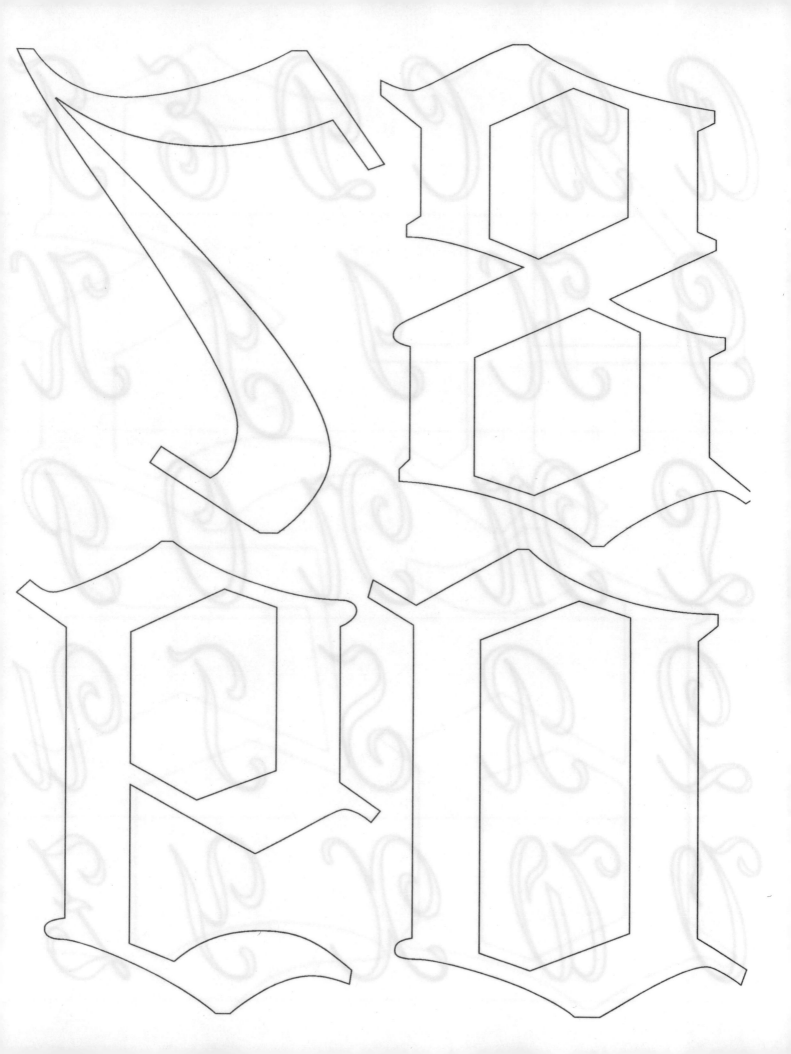

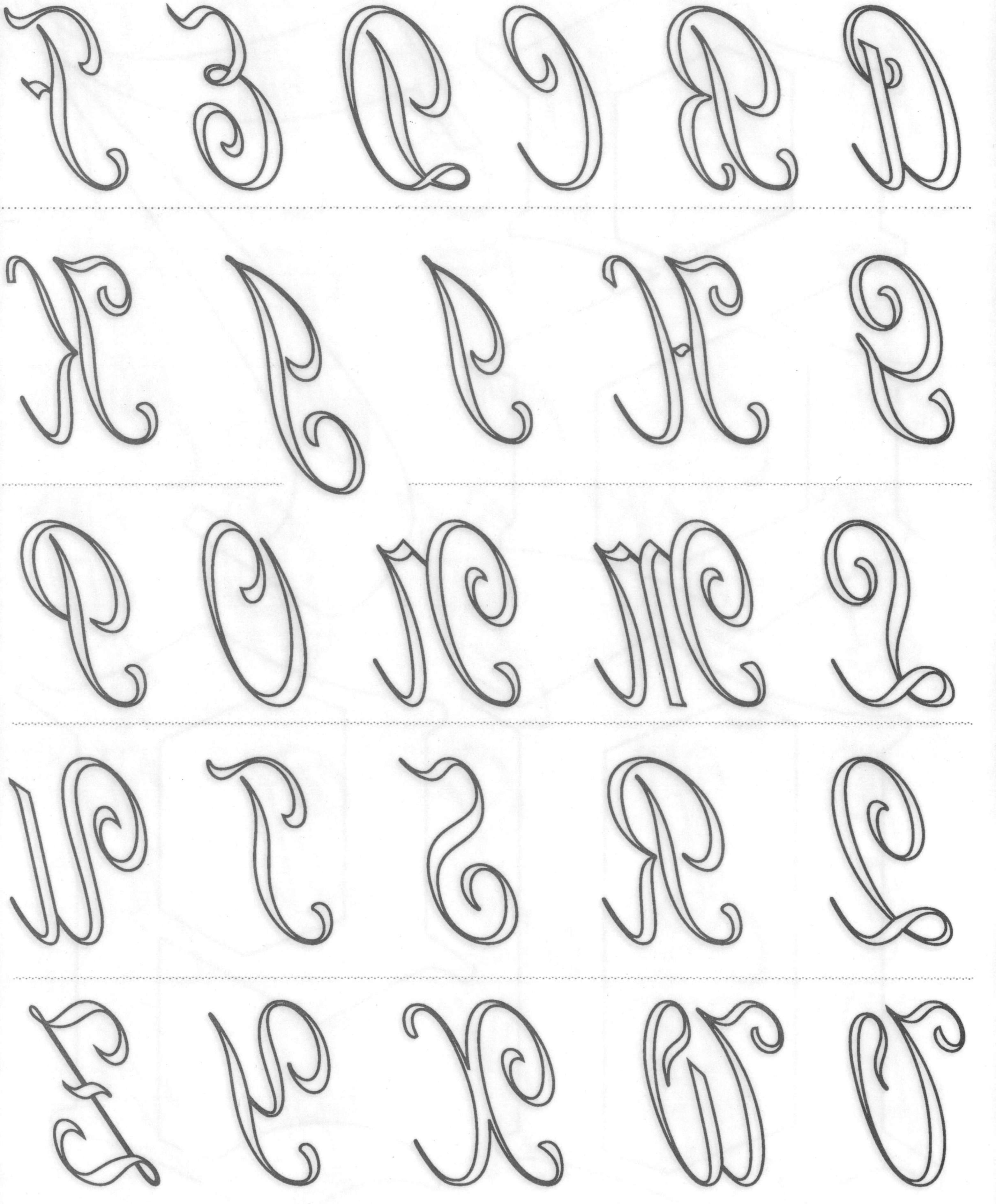

A B C D E F

G H I J K

L M N O P

Q R S T U

V W X Y Z

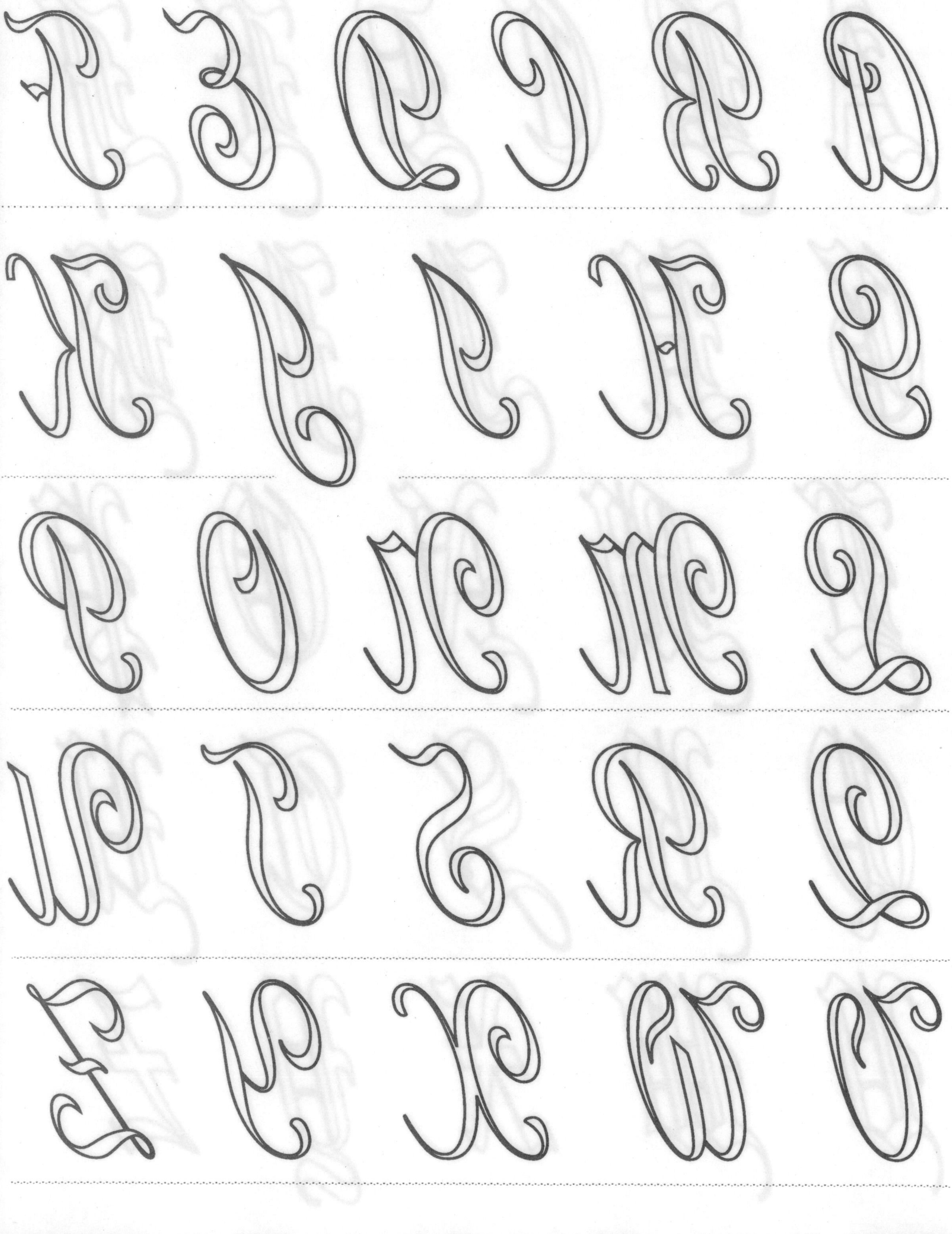

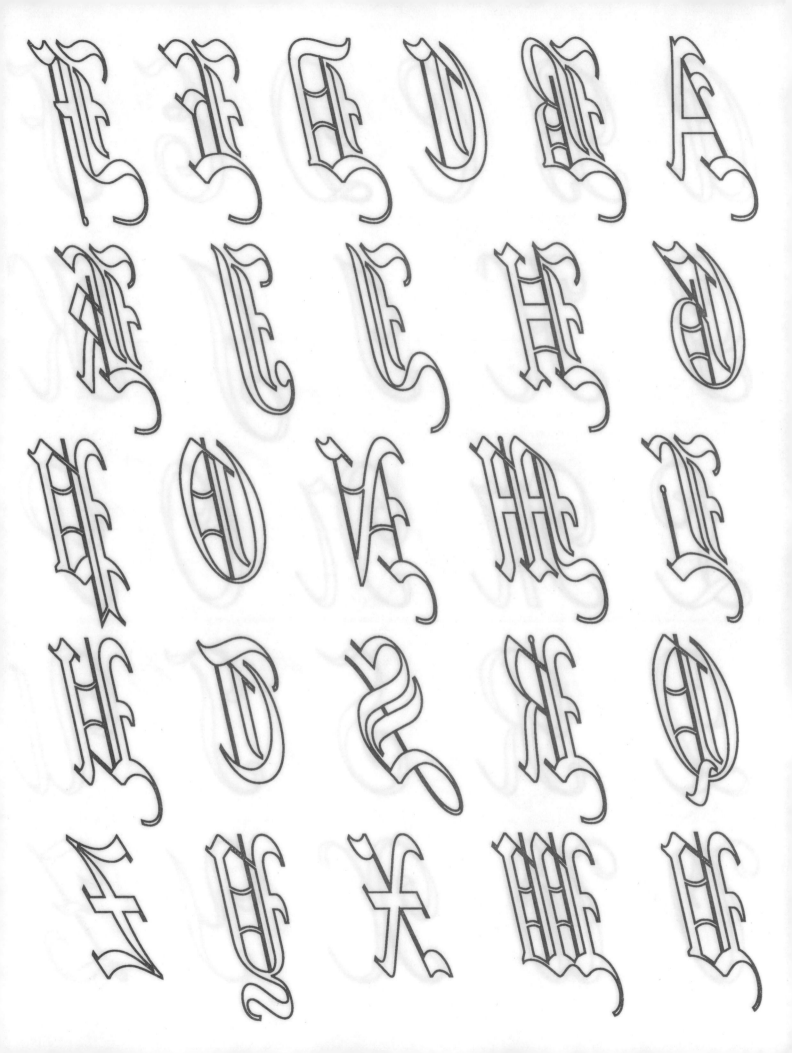

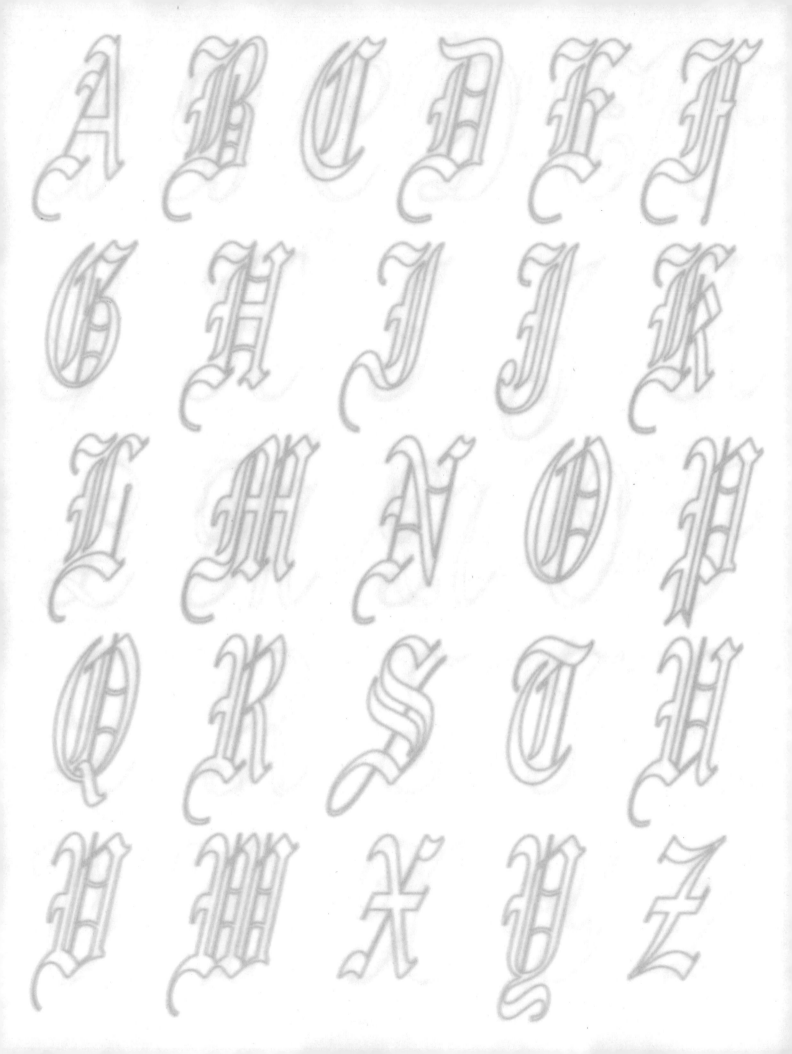

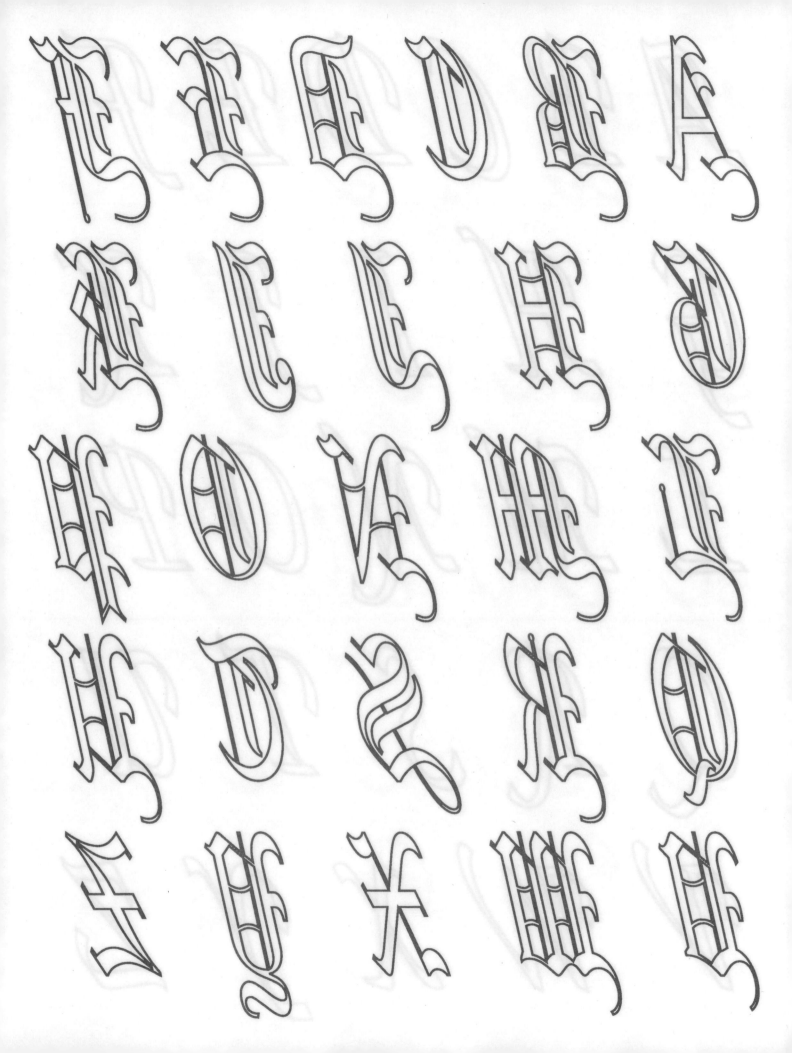

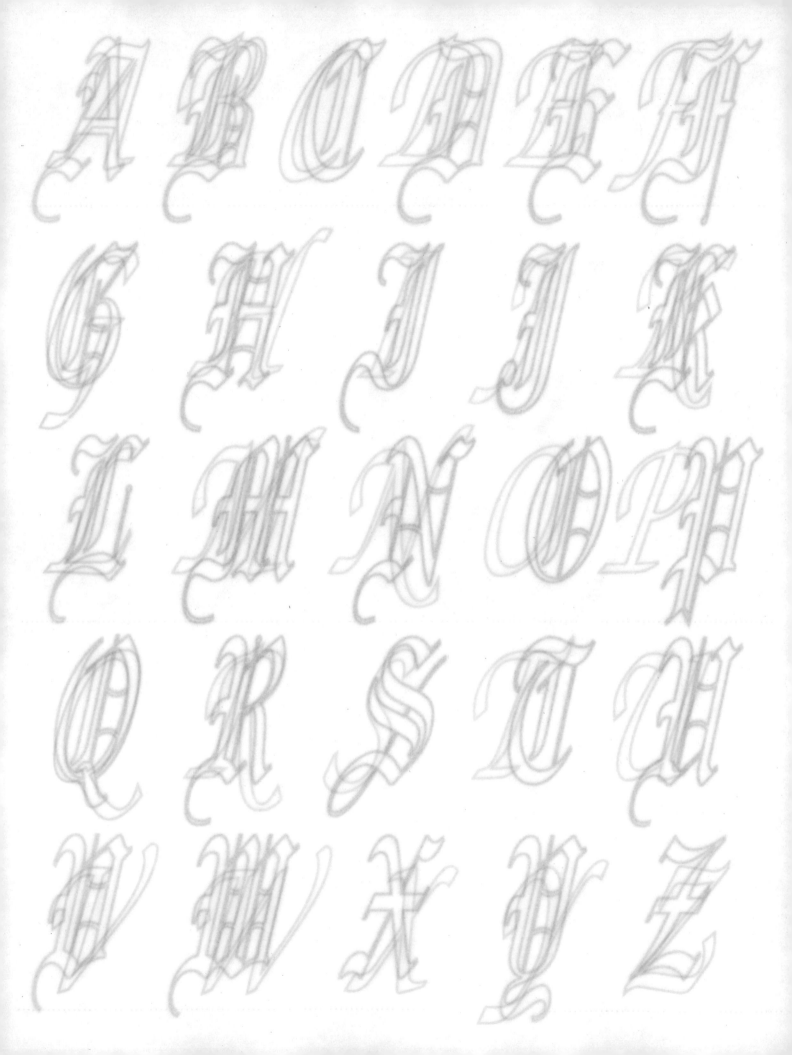

A B C D E F

G H I J K

L M N O P

Q R S T U

V W X Y Z

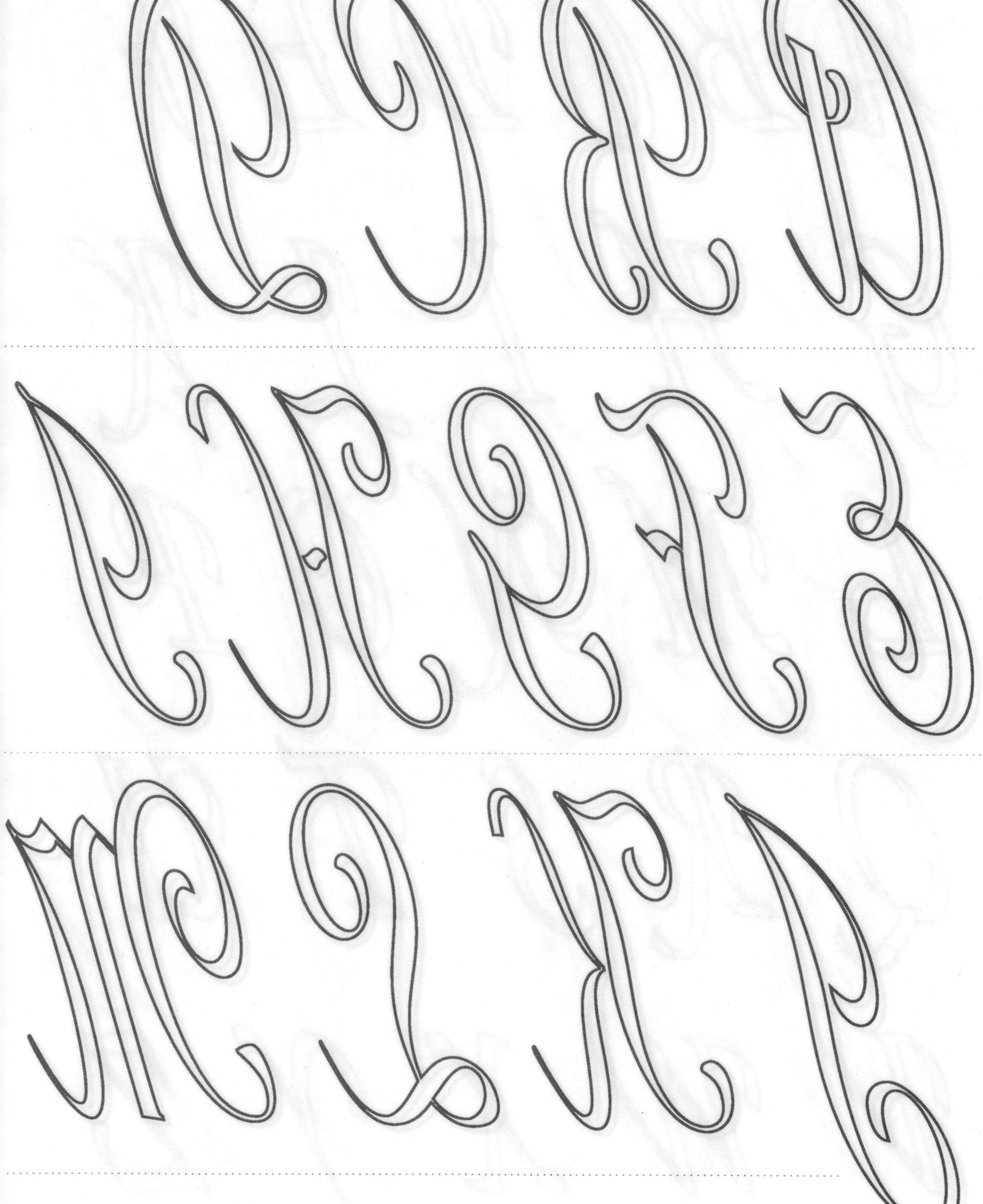

A B C D

E F G H I

J K L M

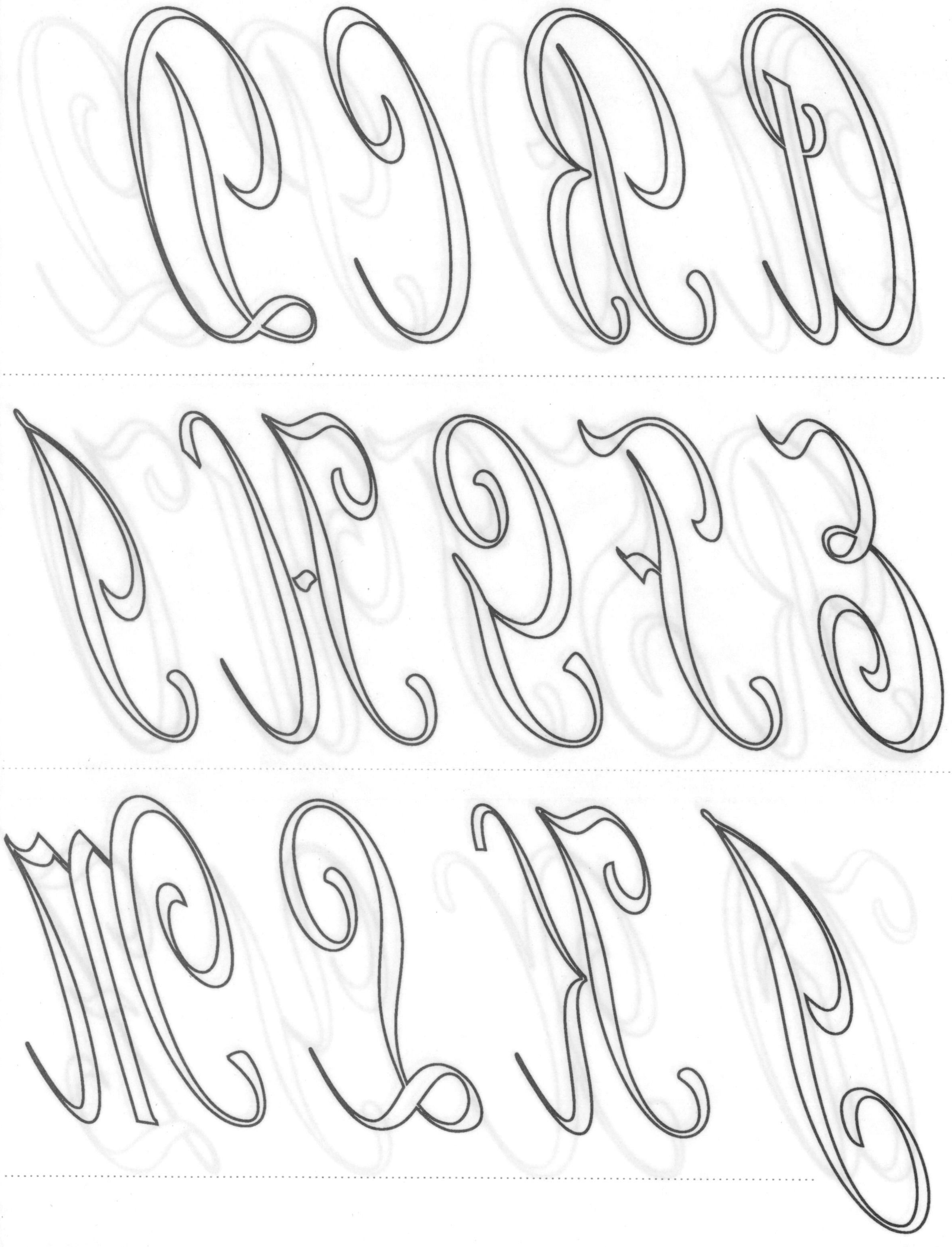

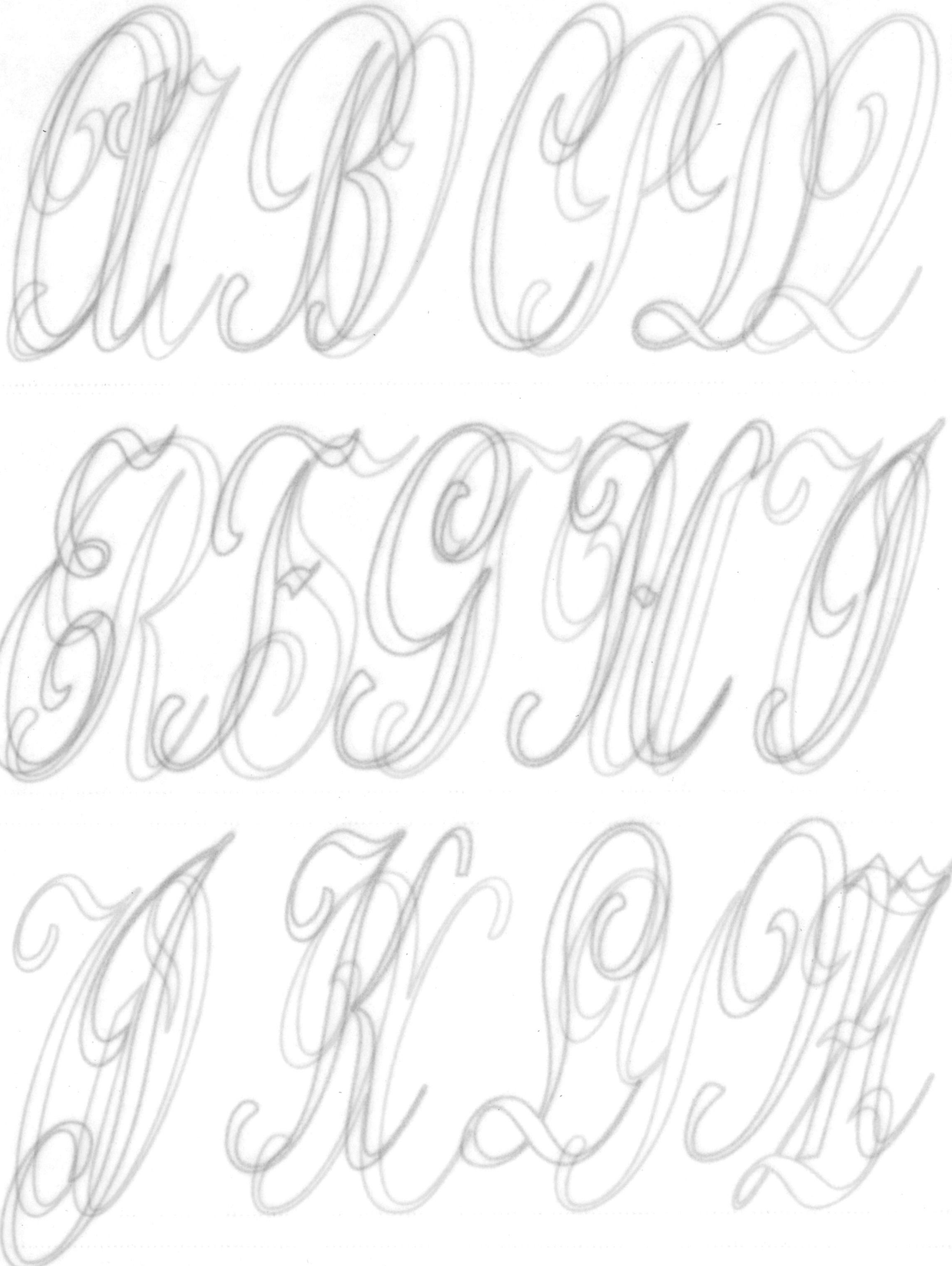
ABCD
EFGHI
JKLM

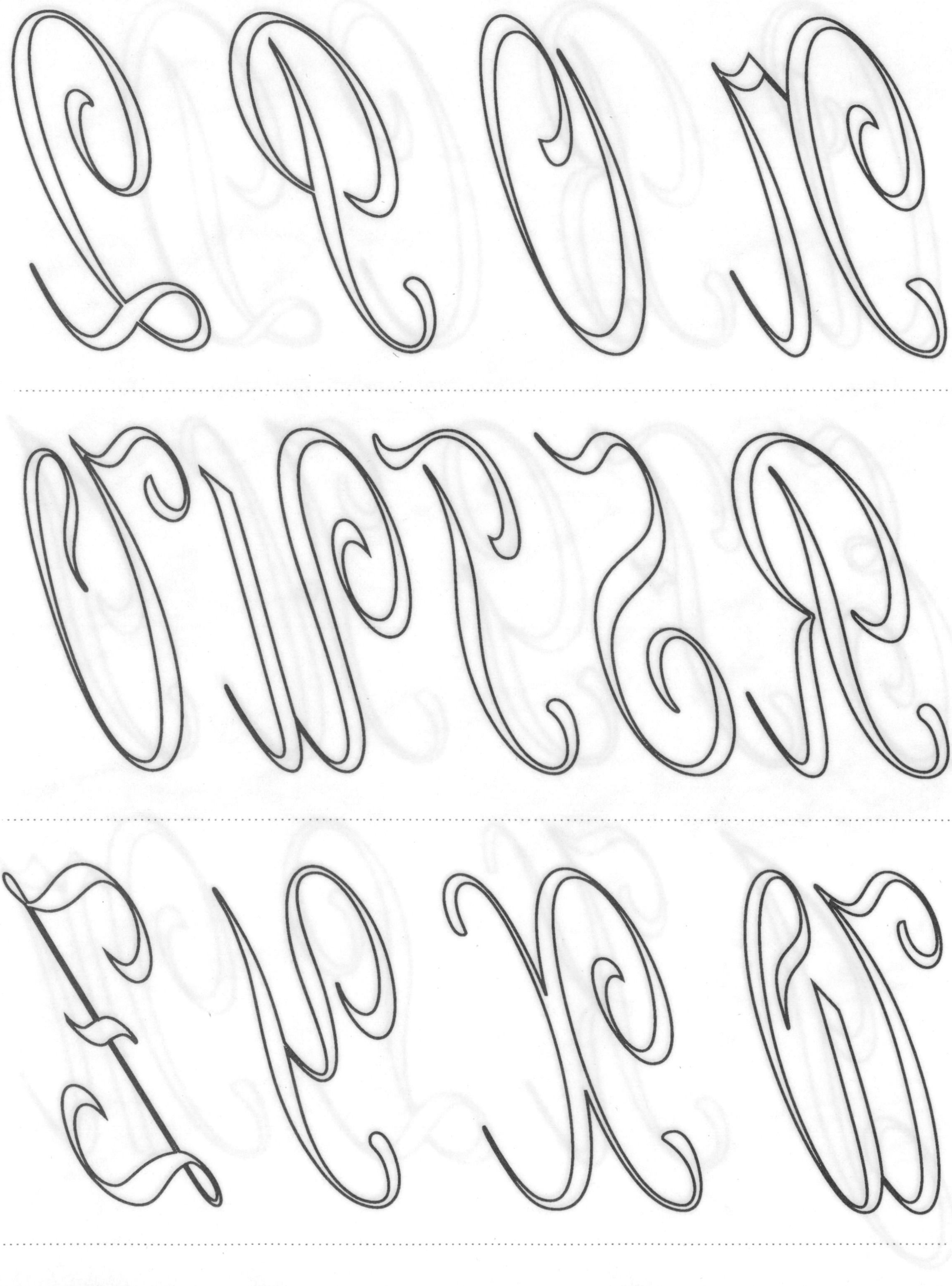

N O P Q

R S T U V

W X Y Z

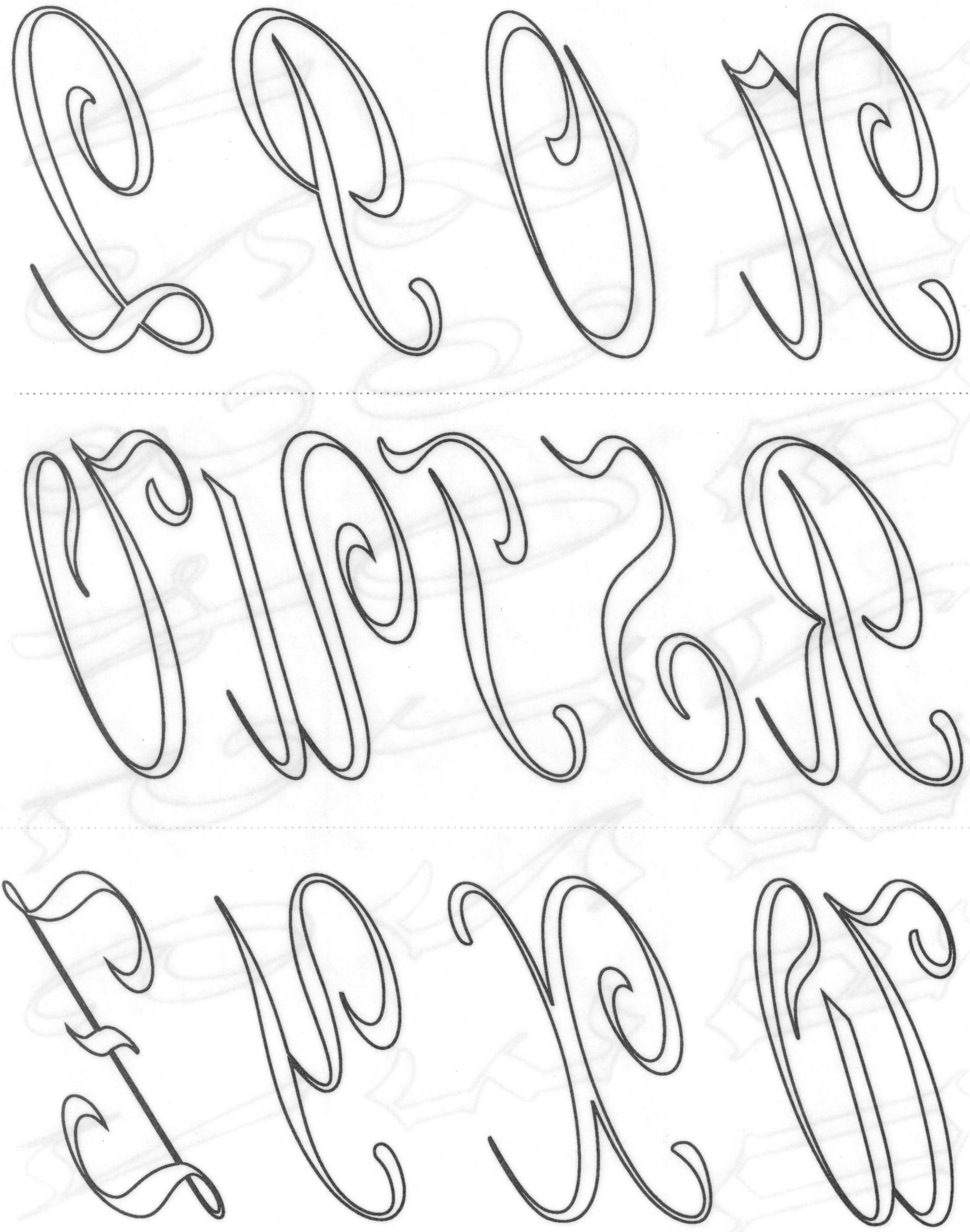

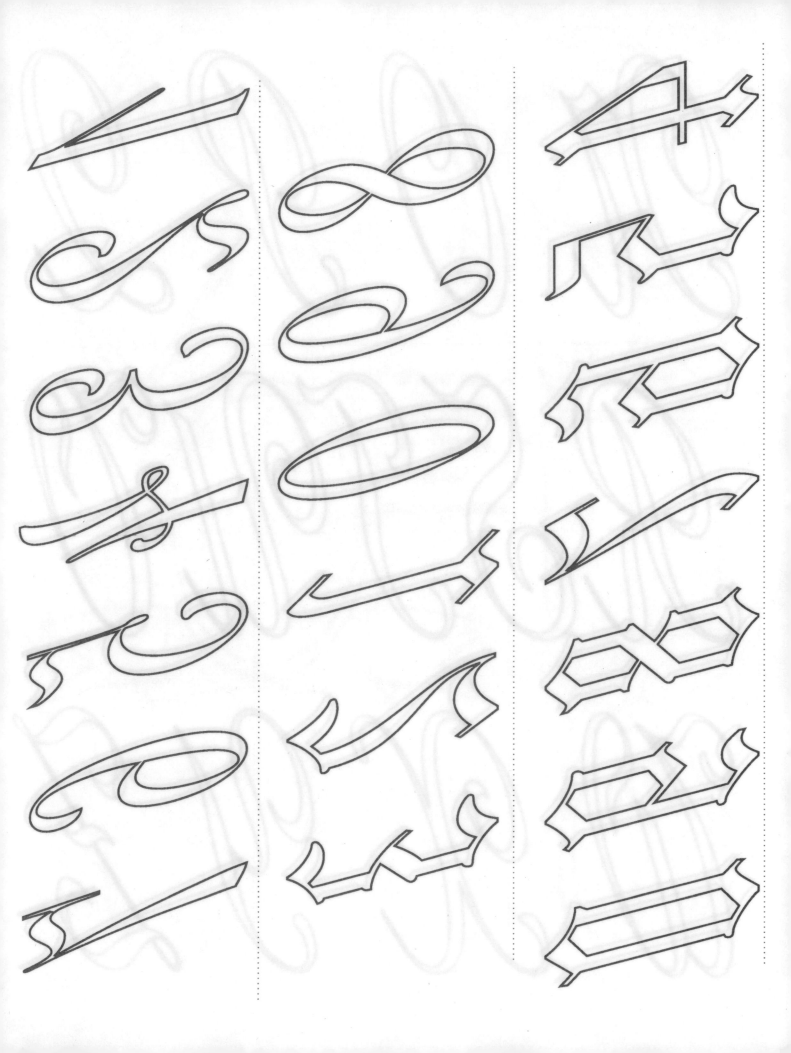

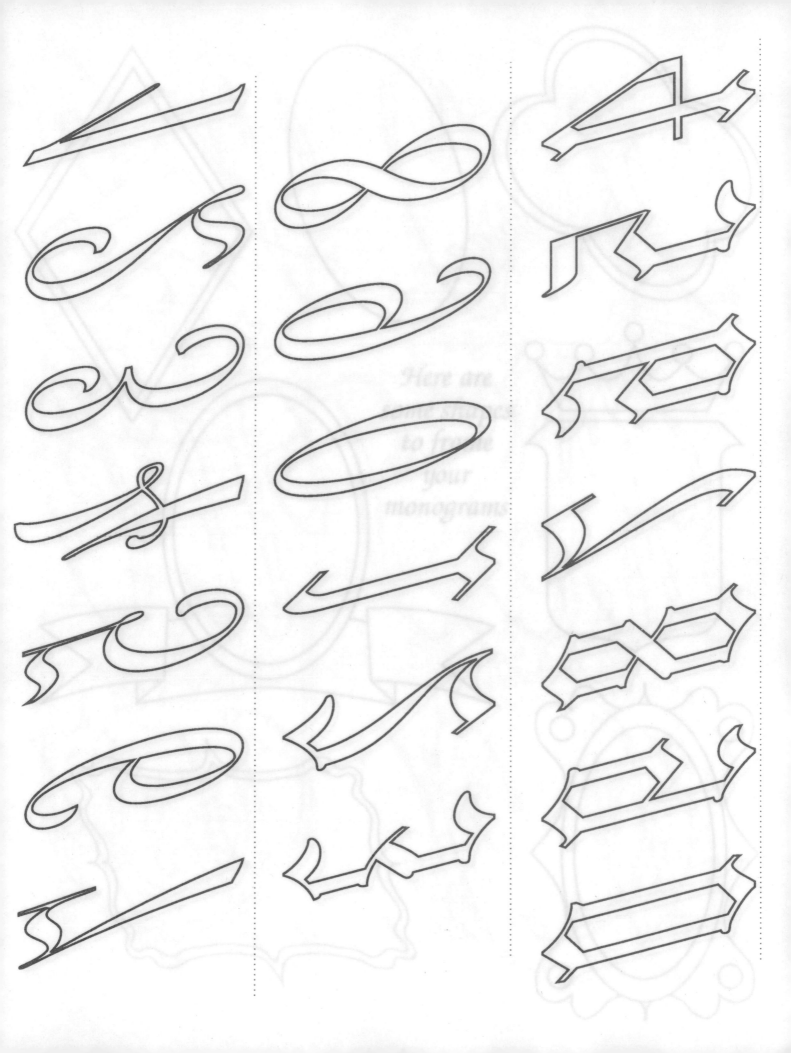

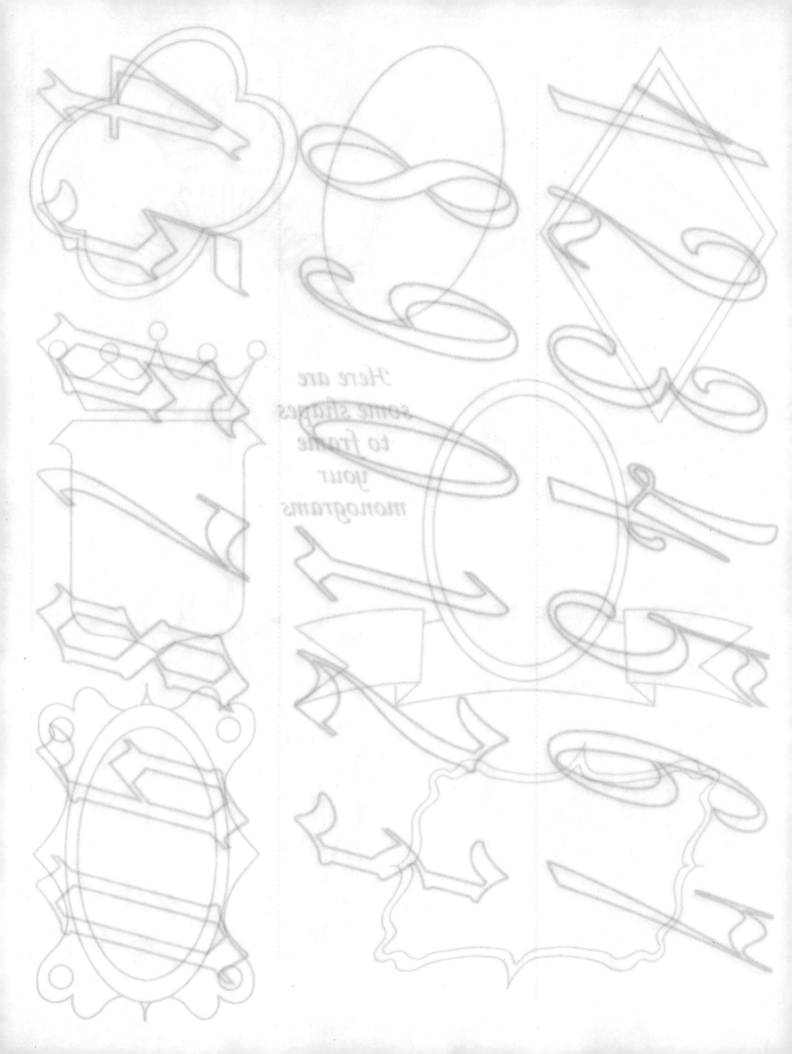

Here are some shapes to frame your monograms

Here are some shapes to frame your monograms

Here are
some shapes
to frame
your
monograms

You can fill in the oval shape with your monogram, color, glitter, jewels or any of the designs on the next page.

A B C D E
F G H I J K
L M N O P
Q R S T U
V W X Y Z

A B C D E

F G H I J K

L M N O P

Q R S T U

V W X Y Z

A B C D E

F G H I J K

L M N O P

Q R S T U

V W X Y Z

A B C D E

F G H I J K

L M N O P

Q R S T U

V W X Y Z